Hannah
Hyphen-Hyphen

Written by Barbara Cooper
Illustrated by Maggie Raynor

GARETH**STEVENS**
GS
PUBLISHING
A World Almanac Education Group Company

Please visit our web site at: **www.garethstevens.com**
For a free color catalog describing Gareth Stevens Publishing's
list of high-quality books and multimedia programs, call
1-800-542-2595 (USA) or 1-800-387-3178 (Canada).
Gareth Stevens Publishing's fax: (414) 332-3567.

Library of Congress Cataloging-in-Publication Data

Cooper, Barbara, 1929-
      [Henrietta Hyphen-Hyphen]
      Hannah Hyphen-Hyphen / written by Barbara Cooper; illustrated by Maggie
Raynor. — North American ed.
         p. cm. — (Meet the Puncs: A remarkable punctuation family)
      Summary: Introduces the use of the hyphen through the story of Hannah,
a member of the Punc family who is high-class and fun-loving.
      ISBN 0-8368-4226-X (lib. bdg.)
      [1. Hyphen—Fiction.   2. English language—Punctuation—Fiction.]
   I. Raynor, Maggie, 1946- , ill.   II. Title.
   PZ7.C78467Han   2004
   [E]—dc22   2004045321

This edition first published in 2005 by
Gareth Stevens Publishing
A World Almanac Education Group Company
330 West Olive Street, Suite 100
Milwaukee, Wisconsin 53212 USA

This U.S. edition copyright © 2005 by Gareth Stevens, Inc. Original edition
copyright © 2003 by Compass Books Ltd., UK. First published in 2003 as
(The Puncs) an adventure in punctuation: Henrietta Hyphen-Hyphen by Compass
Books Ltd.

Designed and produced by Allegra Publishing Ltd., London
Gareth Stevens editor: Dorothy L. Gibbs
Gareth Stevens art direction: Tammy West

Printed in the United States of America

1 2 3 4 5 6 7 8 9 08 07 06 05 04

Hannah Hyphen

is a high‑class Punc who often hob‑nobs with royalty at her estate, known as Hyphen‑on‑the‑Hill.

Her whole name is actually Hannah Anne‑Marie Hyphen‑Hyphen.

chin‑chin

Lord Hobart Punc Hyphen ▬ Hyphen
(1066 ▬ 1120)

Her father, Lieutenant-Colonel Henry Hyphen-Hyphen is a well-known racehorse trainer. Henry is a descendant of Lord Hobart Punc Hyphen-Hyphen of Puncknowle, an 11th-century castle in southwest England.

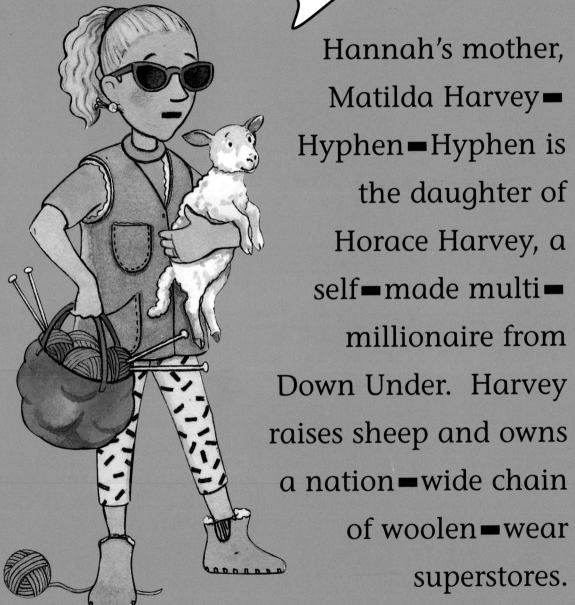

Hannah's mother, Matilda Harvey▬Hyphen▬Hyphen is the daughter of Horace Harvey, a self▬made multi▬millionaire from Down Under. Harvey raises sheep and owns a nation▬wide chain of woolen▬wear superstores.

Hannah is
a first-class
horseback-
competition rider.
She travels,
year-round,
in her horse
trailer to one-day,
two-day, and
three-day events.

She started riding, when, as a five—year—old, she joined the Punc Pony Club. Hannah's first pony, Higgledy—Piggledy, or H—P for short, was three—quarters Pinto and one—quarter Chincoteague.

Hannah and H—P were first—place prizewinners in their very first contest.

Hannah is now a top—notch cross—country rider. You should see her tackle the Double—Hyphen and other fences.

Her skill is mind—boggling. It is not surprising that she and her much—loved ten—year—old, liver—chestnut, quarter horse, Jack—in—the—Box, won the World Punc Three—Day Event.

When she's not competing, you'll often find Hannah working nonstop, 11 a.m.— 6 p.m., at the stables, making sure the horses are spick—and—span and the yard is in apple—pie order.

To help out, Hannah has a bright-eyed, devil-may-care hired-hand named Bobbie-Jo, who sees to the day-to-day running of the Hyphen-Hyphen stables at Punc-on-the-Green.

Bobbie‐Jo looks after Hannah's pets, too: Dum‐Dum, a well‐behaved wirehaired terrier; Riff‐Raff, a sweet‐tempered, curly‐coated retriever; and Ga‐Ga, a potbellied pig, who, by the way, is a real greedy‐gus.

As you probably have noticed by now, high=class Hannah is still a hardworking, team=minded, levelheaded Punc. She also has a very light=hearted side, and she especially enjoys get=togethers and sing=alongs.

Like all weight-watching women, Hannah is careful about what she eats. She will, however, treat herself to an occasional plate of an old English dish called toad-in-the-hole, with a lemon-lime beverage and a whipped-cream-covered black-cherry pastry.

Hannah's good-
looking boyfriend,
Jean-Luc, is a
member of the
highly-thought-of
French family, the
Point-de-Puncs.

Jean—Luc is a fast—riding, tip—top, steeplechase jockey. His favorite horse, Vive—les—Puncs, is a French—bred, dapple—gray gelding.

Besides being all—around horse lovers, Hannah and Jean—Luc like lots of other sports.

In the wintertime, they often go cross—country skiing, and they spend many summer vacations skin—diving in the palm—fringed, blue—green waters around Great Punc Reef.

Hannah thinks Jean-Luc is first-rate, but she is much too happy-go-lucky, right now, to settle down with him or anyone else.

Hannah is very Punc-minded and, for the time being, she just wants to be a world-class, trophy-winning Hyphen-Hyphen.

Pride-of-the-Puncs

It is not hard to see that Hannah is a top—drawer, no—nonsense Punc. Although she can sometimes be a bit high—minded, she is also one of the most fun—loving, kind—hearted, and generous—spirited Puncs. Hannah takes great pleasure in bringing words together, throughout the alphabet, from A—frames to X—ray tubes. It's no wonder she is known as The—Pride—of—the—Puncs.

Hannah's Checklist

- A hyphen is often used with prefixes such as *self-*, *well-*, *all-*, *mid-*, and *half-* and is sometimes used to join a single letter with a word:
Hannah is an all-around horseback rider.
A-frame, X-ray tube, T-shirt

- Use a hyphen with double-digit (compound) number words:
forty-six, sixty-three, thirty-two

- . . . and when numbers are used as describing words (adjectives):
Hannah travels to one-day, two-day, and three-day events. Five-year-old Hannah was already riding in competitions. Hannah's horse is one-quarter Chincoteague.

- Use a hyphen to join two or more adjectives that describe a person, place, or thing (noun):
Hannah is a cross-country rider.

- Hyphens are used in some long or unusual names of places:
Hyphen-on-the-Hill

- Hyphens can be used between dates instead of the word "to":
1066–1120 (1066 to 1120)

- Hyphens are often used in people's names:
Jean-Luc Point-de-Punc

- . . . and in pet's names:
Dum-Dum, Riff-Raff, Ga-Ga

- Hyphens are common in long descriptions:
happy-go-lucky, devil-may-care

- . . . and in word combinations that describe place or position:
side-by-side, in-and-out

- Use a hyphen to break a word at the end of a line but break words only between syllables:
ex-tra-or-di-na-ry

- . . . between double letters:
run-ning

- . . . or before "-ing" word endings:
jump-ing

- Try not, however, to split a proper name, even at the end of a line:
Hannah (not Han-nah)

- Divide hyphenated words only at the hyphen:
Horace Harvey's woolen-wear superstores made him a multimillionnaire.